Learning to Read, Step by Step!

Ready to Read   Preschool–Kindergarten
• big type and easy words • rhyme and rhythm • picture clues
For children who know the alphabet and are eager to begin reading.

Reading with Help   Preschool–Grade 1
• basic vocabulary • short sentences • simple stories
For children who recognize familiar words and sound out new words with help.

Reading on Your Own   Grades 1–3
• engaging characters • easy-to-follow plots • popular topics
For children who are ready to read on their own.

Reading Paragraphs   Grades 2–3
• challenging vocabulary • short paragraphs • exciting stories
For newly independent readers who read simple sentences with confidence.

Ready for Chapters   Grades 2–4
• chapters • longer paragraphs • full-color art
For children who want to take the plunge into chapter books but still like colorful pictures.

STEP INTO READING® is designed to give every child a successful reading experience. The grade levels are only guides; children will progress through the steps at their own speed, developing confidence in their reading. The F&P Text Level on the back cover serves as another tool to help you choose the right book for your child.

Remember, a lifetime love of reading starts with a single step!

Visit us on the Web!
StepIntoReading.com
Seussville.com
pbskids.org/catinthehat
treehousetv.com

Educators and librarians, for a variety of teaching tools, visit us at RHTeachersLibrarians.com

Library of Congress Cataloging-in-Publication Data
Rabe, Tish, author.
Planet name game / by Tish Rabe ; based on a television script by Patrick Granleese ; illustrated by Tom Brannon.
  pages cm. — (Step into reading, step 2)
Summary: "The Cat in the Hat, Sally, and Nick visit each of the planets in this book based on an episode of the PBS Kids TV show The Cat in the Hat Knows a Lot About That!" —Provided by publisher.
Audience: Ages 4–6.
ISBN 978-0-553-49732-8 (trade) — ISBN 978-0-375-97373-4 (lib. bdg.)
ISBN 978-0-553-49734-2 (ebook)
1. Cat in the Hat (Fictitious character)—Juvenile literature. 2. Planet—Juvenile literature. 3. Solar system—Juvenile literature. I. Granleese, Patrick. II. Brannon, Tom, illustrator. III. Cat in the hat knows a lot about that! (Television program). IV. Title.
QB602.R315 2015 523.4—dc23 2014006105

Printed in the United States of America
10 9 8 7 6 5 4 3 2 1

This book has been officially leveled by using the F&P Text Level Gradient™ Leveling System.

Planet Name Game

by Tish Rabe
based on a television script by
Patrick Granleese
illustrated by Tom Brannon

Random House 🏠 New York

One day the Cat said,
"Today we will fly
and see all the planets
way up in the sky.

"There are eight planets that circle the sun. We can name them all and have lots of fun.

"First stop is the sun.

Look! Here we are!

Have I told you that

the sun is a star?

"Up in the sky
it may look like a dot.
When we get close,
you can feel it is HOT!

"The first planet we see

is closest to the sun.

It is Mercury.

It is the smallest one.

"We named one planet.
Now what do we do?
Now we blast off for
planet number two!

"This planet is Venus.
It never rains here.
It is dusty and dry
every day of the year.

"This planet is Earth.
We can easily see
why it is called the Blue Planet.
It is Planet Three.

"It has lots of oceans
that make it look blue.
I love this planet!
I bet you do, too!

"Now we will fly
way up past some stars
to the next planet,
the one we call Mars."

"I know that Mars is
the Red Planet," Nick said.
"And I can see why.
It really *is* red!"

"Jupiter," the Cat said,
"is fifth from the sun.
As you can see,
it's the biggest one.

"We can see it is big when we fly beside it. The other planets could all fit inside it!

"This planet is Saturn.
We can see two things.
It's the second biggest
and it has bright rings.

"It is the sixth planet.

There are only two more.

Oh! I think space is

such fun to explore!

"Next is Uranus (YUR-uh-nus).

It has rings, too.

There is just one planet

left to show you.

20

"This planet is Neptune.

It is Planet Eight.

"We did it! Hooray!

This name game is great!

"We named them all.
Our name game is fun.
We can do it again
and start with Planet One!

SOLAR SYSTEM

"We named Mars and then we named Jupiter, too. Saturn was the sixth planet I showed you.

"Uranus, then Neptune . . .

Our name game is done.

Unless—we play it again

and start with . . .

SOLAR SYSTEM

"... the sun!"